Snapchat Is The New Black

The Unrivaled Guide to Snapchat Marketing

acknowledge that the author is not engaging in the rendering of legal, financial, medical or professional advice. The content of this book has been derived from various sources. Please consult a licensed professional before attempting any techniques outlined in this book.

By reading this document, the reader agrees that under no circumstances are is the author responsible for any losses, direct or indirect, which are incurred as a result of the use of information contained within this document, including, but not limited to, —errors, omissions, or inaccuracies.

Table of Contents

Introduction 1

Chapter One: Getting Started With Snapchat.... 3

Chapter Two: Snapchat Features 11

Chapter Three: Basic Snapchat Lingo 19

Chapter Four: Symbols 25

Chapter Five: Advantages of Using Snapchat.. 31

Chapter Six: Snapchat For Business 39

Chapter Seven: Increasing Snapchat followers 45

Chapter Eight: Snapchat and Other Media 53

Chapter Nine: Snapchat Marketing Strategies 59

Chapter Ten: Snapchat Lenses, Filters and
Settings 67

Chapter Eleven: Snapchat Tips and Tricks 73

Chapter Twelve: How Snapchat Can Improve. 85

Summary 93

Conclusion 97

Introduction

Snapchat is now one of the most popular social media platforms in the world and for good reason. Not only does it help in connecting people with friends and family but also keep them updated with the latest photos and videos.

Launched in 2011, Snapchat is meant to serve as a form of picture social media. It encourages people to post their pictures and videos to share with friends and family. These pictures self-destruct after a few seconds of the viewer seeing it thereby making it quite unique.

Despite being extremely popular with teens and young adults, Snapchat can also be used to enhance business potential. It serves as the

Introduction

perfect promotional tool to sell products and services.

Many companies, big and small, now rely on it to sell their products. If you happen to be one such business house looking to tap into the app's popularity then this is the right book for you. It will guide you through the details of the app, and tell you how useful it is for both regular people and businesses. We will look at how one can get started with Snapchat and how a business house can use it to its advantage.

If you are not on Snapchat then you are missing out on a lot of fun! Once you are done with this book, you will be raring to put it to good use! So hop on board to have an insight of how useful the app really can be.

Chapter One:

Getting Started With Snapchat

W elcome to the first chapter of this book. In this first chapter, we will look at the basics of Snapchat and how to get started with the app.

What is Snapchat?

Snapchat is a social media app that was launched in 2011 with the intention of helping people share photos and videos that self-destruct within minutes of the receiver receiving it. This feature is unique to Snapchat and helps people maintain privacy. Ever since its launch, Snapchat has grown in popularity and is now one of the most widely used social media apps in the world. Available on all mobile platforms, it is an app designed to help people express themselves better. Right from celebrities to famous personalities, everybody has joined the Snapchat bandwagon thereby enhancing its overall appeal. Snapchat is easy to download and easier to use.

When was it launched?

Snapchat was launched in 2011 and has since had many updates. The current version is extremely popular and designed to suit a vast number of people. As per statistics, more than 700 million snaps are shared per day on Snapchat with an average of 9000 pics being shared every second thus making it extremely popular. It is regarded as the best app to send and receive pictures. The app was offered to be absorbed by Facebook but the creators declined, as they did not want to be a part of a commercial vehicle. Facebook then tried to launch a rival app called slingshot that failed to match up to Snapchat's popularity.

What is its purpose?

In this day and age where everybody is interested in sharing pictures and videos, it is obvious that an app dedicated to the cause makes for the perfect choice. But for most people these days, privacy issues are a big worry making it tough for them to confidently share their pictures with others, and that is exactly where Snapchat capitalized. It was launched with the intention of helping people share their pictures with others without being worried about privacy. The pictures self-destruct within seconds thereby not giving the other person a chance to keep it. This is the app's biggest selling point.

Who can use Snapchat?

Snapchat was originally launched to appeal to teens and young adults. The app has features such as the addition of filters that can be used to modify and enhance the quality of pictures. This became an instant hit with college and office goers. However, with time, businesses began to

5

realize Snapchat's worth as a means to promote their products and services. They began using the app to their advantage as it was dubbed as a great way to increase a brand's popularity. Many business houses now rely on Snapchat to expand their customer base and increase sales. You too can avail the same by reading the different tips and tricks mentioned in this book.

How does Snapchat work?

Snapchat is regarded as one of the best apps to use to keep in touch with family and friends. It is a simple application that allows users to share pictures and videos with ease. It also provides a platform for people to chat with each other. This makes it convenient for people to keep in touch and share pictures and videos with each other. A person's friends and followers will be able to look at the pictures and videos that the person has shared and share their own with their followers.

Getting started with Snapchat

It is easy to get started with Snapchat by following a few basic steps. Here is looking at them.

1. Step 1: the very first step is to download the app from the app store. It is available on android, iOS and windows store. Once the app downloads, you have to open it on your phone.

2. Step 2: Once you do, it will ask you to fill in the email, password and birthday. These details will be mandatory to fill in. You will have to be at least 13 years of age to use the app otherwise you will be redirected to what is known as snapkidz.

3. Step 3: the app will then identify your identity by asking a few questions. These are simple questions that are mostly visual in nature.

4. Step 4: The next step is to add contacts to your list. Snapchat will ask to access your contact list. Doing so will help you transfer all your contacts to your Snapchat. But if you don't want to do so then can modify the friend list and add only those that you wish to have on your list.

5. Step 5: the next step is to pick your personal preferences. You have the option of managing the filters, the camera flash, reply tab, special text etc. You have the option to choose who can send you pictures and who to receive from.

6. Step 6: The next step is to use the camera to take snaps. These snaps can be shared with others. The app will automatically access your camera to take the pictures. You have the choice to add a tagline or caption to the photo to personalize it. There are also many filters to choose from

that will enhance the appeal of the pictures.

7. Step 7: the next step is to send the snap to the person you wish to share it with. Choose from the list of friends and send it over.

8. Step 8: you will also be able to receive snaps. Go to the received snaps to find the pictures that were sent.

9. Step 9: you have the choice to add a story. A story can be a video or picture to tell your followers know what you have been up to. A story lasts 24 hours and then self-destructs.

10. Step 10: start a chat session with a friend. This feature is like any other chat messenger. The messages will be placed one above the other.

Chapter One: Getting Started With Snapchat

These form the different steps to follow in order to get started with Snapchat. It is pretty simple and has been designed to make it easier for people to share pictures and start conversations.

Chapter Two:

Snapchat Features

Snapchat comes with many different features. It has been designed to convenience people and enhances their social media experience. Here is locking at some of the prominent features of Snapchat. These are the new features that come with the latest version of the app.

Profile Picture

You have the option of adding your picture in the center of the Snapchat icon. To add a picture go to your profile page and tap on the ghost icon. Once the camera switches on, take the picture. This picture will be used as your profile and will be visible to whoever is following your profile. In fact, you can take a series of shots that will appear in loop as your profile picture.

Chat Feature

The chat feature on Snapchat is designed to help people chat conveniently. The buttons on the interface includes a photo button on the leftmost corner followed by a phone button followed by a snap button followed by a video button followed by a sticker button. The photo button helps you send photos and videos to a friend. These will be from your phone's library. The phone button is designed to help you make voice calls. The snap button helps you take a snap and send it across. The video button is designed to make video calls. The sticker button helps you add stickers to pictures and all of these options together make it a great chatting app, ideal for teens and adults.

Video Messages

The app is a great place to send and receive video messages. It is also serves as a good platform to share video calls with friends and family. Just choose the video button and you will be able to send a video or make a video call. The video call feature is great, as it provides you with many different options. If you have a stable Internet connection then you can make a video call to your friend. If you don't wish to turn your video on then can simply choose to watch the call and have the other person's video play as you chat and vice versa. It is also easy to leave voice messages for your friends and family. This makes the app extremely versatile and ideal for a whole host of people.

Autoplay

A new feature with Snapchat is Autoplay. Autoplay automatically moves you the next story without you having to move yourself. As soon as you are done watching a friend's story, Snapchat will automatically move you to the next one and so on. This is different from when you would be directed to the main story page after finishing a story. This feature makes it convenient for a lot of people who do not wish to manually move pages. If you do not wish to make use of this feature then you have the choice to just pull down and stop Autoplay.

Campus Stories

This feature is exclusively designed for students. This allows students in a particular campus to create and receive stories. These stories will help you keep tab of what others are doing on a day-to-day basis. These will come through if you were on a particular campus in the recent past. They will automatically disappear within 24 hours. Although some privacy concerns were raised about the same, the issue has been fixed with the latest version of the app. This is a convenient way for people to create and share stories with their friends and people on your list.

Snap Streak

A snap streak refers to the time period for which you and a friend have sent each other snaps. It is designed to remind you to send each other snaps on a daily basis. After all, the app is meant to share pictures and so will be important to do so as much as possible. You have the choice to send whatever picture you like without worrying about the content. If in case you miss out on a day and lose the streak then can consider reaching out to the support team for help.

Geofilters

Geofilters are the images that can be placed over your pictures. This is a great little feature as it helps in personalizing your pictures. You also have the chance to create your own filters that can be used to create unique pictures. There is also the option to use lenses. These lenses help with creating unique pictures. Although some lenses were once chargeable, they are now free to use. This is a welcome change for many as the lenses prove to be a fun little feature of the app. However, the lenses keep changing on a regular basis and do not remain the same for long.

Chapter Two: Snapchat Features

Browsing

Browsing through the snaps is now quite easy. There are fun options available to choose from that will move the snaps as per your liking. The first option is moving slowly and is represented by a snail icon. The second option is moving faster and represented by a rabbit. The last option is three arrows pointing backwards to represent rewind. Using these makes it fun to watch snaps, stories and videos on Snapchat.

Changing Profile Emojis

You have the option of changing the profiles of your friends. It will automatically set emojis next to your friend's names but you will have the choice of changing it to whatever emoji you like. There are many options to pick from and can choose whatever emoji you think fits the person best. To change the emojis go to settings, Additional Services, Manage and then Friends emojis. There you will be able to make the changes.

These form some of the unique features of Snapchat that make it a simple yet great social media app to use.

Chapter Three:

Basic Snapchat Lingo

S napchat has its own lingo that helps people communicate better with each other. You need to be aware of the same in order to.

Snaps

Snaps refer to the individual pictures that are shared in Snapchat. They are what will be shared with friends and family members. You send across snaps to Snapchatters, which is the term referred for people who use Snapchat. These snaps will last for a maximum of 10 seconds before being destroyed. You will also be given the option to choose an appropriate time lesser than 10 seconds to view the snaps.

Chapter Three: Basic Snapchat Lingo

Snapback

Snapback refers to the replies given to a snap. In other words, a snapback is the response provided by people to other snaps. You will have the chance to measure the number of snapbacks that you have given out and the people who received it.

Story

A story is a series of pictures or snaps that one can add to their Snapchat account. They can be played in loop by your followers in as many times as they like within 24 hours of uploading it. Each story can be a narrative of an event that you were part of, the previous day. You can view your friend's stories in the story section of your account.

Scores

Scores are unique statistics that are provided to an individual based on the number of snaps shared, received, snapbacks etc. All of these are taken into account to provide a unique score to an individual. You have the option to check your friends' scores as well to know how many snaps they have sent and received.

Snapcode

Snapcodes are a convenient way to add new friends. Use your phone to scan and add new friends to your account. It is both simple and easy to do so. Access your Snapcode by tapping on the ghost icon.

Snapstreak

Snapstreak refers to the consecutive days when you shared snaps with a friend. It is important to keep sharing as many photos as possible since that is the main feature of the app.

Friends and Followers

There is a difference between friends and followers on your account. Friends refer to the people who have been added from your phone contact list. You will be given the option to add them that will appear on the right most corners. Followers on the other hand are people that are following you but you are not following them. They will show up on your list of followers.

Lenses

Lenses refer to the modifications that you can make to the pictures. They are real time effects that can be added to your snaps. There are many filters to choose from and each one is unique. These lenses are now free of cost and can be used to modify pictures. They change everyday so you won't get bored with them.

Filters

Filters are overlays that go on top of your pictures. These are meant to make your pictures interesting. There are many fun filters to choose from with each one providing a different effect. Geofilters are especially popular as they allow you to place fun pictures on your photos.

FTFY

FTFY stands for fixed that for you. It means that you fix something for someone. It is literally said as a means to apologize for something that was done unintentionally. It is also used as a means to signify a modification to a picture.

HIFW

HIFW refers to how i felt when. It is meant to signify a feeling that was felt. This is generally used to signify a humorous situation.

JSYK

This is an alternate to FYI and stands for just so you know. It is said to inform someone something they should know.

MIRK

MIRK stands for me in real life. This is used in humor to signify a funny incident. It is supplemented with a funny picture or snap.

Chapter Three: Basic Snapchat Lingo

NSFW

NSFW stands for not safe for work. It is supplemented with pictures that cannot be opened at work because they can get you in trouble.

SMH

SMH stands for shaking my head, as a means to signify something you shared is funny or silly. It is generally said in a humorous way.

TIL

TIL stands for today I learned. It is used to signify that you learned something new.

These form the various short forms used on Snapchat. Using them will save your time and make it easier for you to communicate.

Chapter Four:

Symbols

Snapchat uses many different symbols to signify specific messages. Here are some of them and their meanings.

➢ A pink opaque box means you have an unopened message waiting for you.

➢ A purple opaque box means you have an unopened video snap waiting for you.

➢ A blue opaque box means you have an unread text message waiting for you.

➢ An empty pink box means you have opened the picture snap.

➢ An empty purple box means you have opened the video snap.

Chapter Four: Symbols

- ➢ An empty blue box means you have opened a text chat.

- ➢ An opaque pink arrow means a friend has not yet seen your snap.

- ➢ An opaque purple arrow means friend has not yet opened a video snap.

- ➢ An opaque blue arrow means friend has not yet opened a text message.

- ➢ An empty pink arrow means friend has opened the snap.

- ➢ An empty purple arrow means friend has opened video snap.

- ➢ An empty blue arrow means a friend has opened the text message.

- ➢ A cake symbol means it's your friend's birthday.

Common Myths

Snapchat is not for businesses

This is a very common misconception that surrounds Snapchat. People believe that Snapchat is exclusively designed for people and that it will not work for businesses. However, this is only a myth as it is great for businesses to promote their products and services. Companies will find it convenient to come up with strategies using pictures and videos to reach out to an audience. Through the course of this book we will look at the many ways in which you can use Snapchat for business purposes.

Snapchat is overshadowed by other platforms

This is another misconception doing the rounds. People believe that Snapchat is not as popular as Facebook or twitter. But this is a wrong comparison as they are not all the same. Facebook and twitter are different from

Chapter Four: Symbols

Snapchat in that they are used to promote messages. Snapchat on the other hand is exclusively for picture promotions. This works better as people will be drawn to pictures as compared to just text. Snapchat is in a league of its own and not affected by competition from other sites.

Snapchat does not allow marketing

Snapchat has a feature known as story telling where people can add in a series of pictures to tell a story. This feature is great as companies can post a series of pictures about a campaign or even their products. This allows them to market their products effectively. It is a great tool to use to send across a message to the audience, as they will be able to relate to it better. In fact, many companies, big and small, now use Snapchat stories as a means to campaign their products.

It will take time to establish oneself

This will depend on the type of campaigns that are being used. If the campaigns are interesting and you manage to score a lot of followers then you will establish yourself pretty quickly. You must ensure that you keep your content up to date and provide your audiences with interesting material. Only then will you be able to capitalize on Snapchat's success as a promotional tool. Snapchat is still relatively new to the world of business promotion and does not promote it as aggressively as Facebook and twitter so it will take a little time for you to use Snapchat to promote business.

I am on Instagram so I don't need Snapchat

Instagram and Snapchat are not the same. In fact, they are extremely diverse and do not clash on any level. Snapchat provides you with a platform where pictures are automatically destroyed after a certain point of time. This

Chapter Four: Symbols

makes it ideal for many types of businesses and allows them to come up with new campaigns every now and then. The features provided on Snapchat are also quite different from the ones on Instagram. So if you want a great platform to promote your business then Snapchat is the one for you.

Chapter Five:

Advantages of Using Snapchat

Snapchat is easily the best photo-sharing app out there. There are hundreds of advantages of using it and some of them are discussed in this chapter.

Point of view

One of the biggest advantages of using Snapchat is that it helps people give others a first hand perspective of their world. Friends and family members will be able to see what you see and how you see it. This will bring you closer and help share more information with each other. Other people will be able to see what you are seeing at the exact moment thereby making it extremely special for both.

Chapter Five: Advantages of Using Snapchat

Timing

The fact that Snapchat stories last just 24 hours makes it convenient for many people. It is best for those that do not wish to maintain too many videos and pictures. They will be able to do away with their snaps that will self-destruct within the designated time. It is also great for those that wish to maintain their privacy. The pictures will not remain long enough for the other person to misuse it. Even if they screenshot it, you will be notified about the same.

Buzz

It is a great platform to create a buzz. The app allows you to create short videos that will act as a teaser for others. They will have a short preview of it that will create a buzz among your followers. It is a great way to generate interest among people and other social media platforms. This especially works well for those that wish to promote themselves and their business. It is also possible to make viral videos. It makes it quite easy to build up an audience without much effort.

Ease

It is extremely easy to use Snapchat, which is one of its biggest advantages. It is easy to download the app and start using it to share pictures and chat. It is a small file and will not eat away into your phone's memory. The user interface of the app is great and user friendly. Snapchat is great for teens and adults that wish to keep in touch with their friends and family.

Snapchat for business

Snapchat is a great new way for businesses to increase their reach and enhance business opportunity. Here is looking at the many ways in which businesses can make use of Snapchat for their advantage.

- Snapchat is a great platform for live event coverage. Businesses have the chance to cover events live as a means to reach out to a big audience. For example the audience can be made a part of live contests and events. NBA used the app in 2014 to allow the audience a chance to take part in live draft picking. Similarly, businesses can involve their audiences in live events. This is a great way to keep them interested and increase the audience base.

- Many companies these days use Snapchat as a means to create a buzz for their products and services. This helps with increasing people's interest. They release a small trailer of what is to come in order to intrigue people and get them to follow. It can go a long way in increasing the audience's intrigue and making it fun and exciting. Older companies looking to connect with the newer audiences can use this technique.

- In fact, the average age group of users is 13 to 34 years, which means that it is easier to connect with the youngsters. It is also the hardest age group to please and Snapchat will make it easier for companies to reach out to them and cater to their changing tastes. Companies such as cover girl regularly use Snapchat to increase customer base and reach out to their target audiences.

- Many companies use Snapchat to post what goes on behind the scenes. With the Internet proving to be a very entertaining platform, more and more companies are aiming at using Snapchat to help the audience feel connected. Companies such as Everlane use Snapchat to post pictures of whatever is going on behind the scenes of the company. This makes it interesting and fun for the audience.

- Snapchat is a great platform for businesses to offer giveaways. Everybody loves giveaways as it makes the audience feel special. Snapchat makes for a good platform, as companies are able to offer their audiences a chance to win something for themselves. Many cosmetic companies are known to use Snapchat as a means to give away products to their customers and followers.

- There are a lot of features that can be used to leverage audience reach. Some of this includes checking the total unique views. This is used to check how many customers and followers have checked Snapchat within a specified period of time. The next metric is checking total story completions. This is to see whether people are viewing the entire story. This will tell you to make it shorter or longer. The last statistic to check will be to see whether customers are taking screenshots. Although Snapchat is not designed to allow people to do so, this feature comes in very handy for businesses that can check how many people are screen shooting.

These are just some of the advantages of using Snapchat for business and are not limited to just these. The others will automatically come through as and when you use Snapchat.

Chapter Six:

Snapchat For Business

Snapchat is extremely useful for business houses as it provides a great platform to retain customers and find new ones. It is understood that it was launched with teens and young adults in mind but soon became popular as a means to promote products and services.

Here is looking at how Snapchat is great for businesses.

➢ It is no secret that Snapchat is now one of the most widely used social medias in the world. With an estimated 100 million active users, it is easily the best platform for a business house to promote its products and services.

➢ But not all companies think of it as a platform to promote themselves since they prefer Facebook or Twitter. As per studies only 2% of the top companies use Snapchat for advertising meaning there is a lot of scope for an upcoming business to use it to its advantage.

➢ Upcoming businesses will especially benefit from this fact, as they will not be part of the rat race. It is also ideal for businesses that are already established but looking for a fresh source to find the right audiences. Many established companies are now turning to Snapchat because of the big opportunity that it provides in terms of increasing sales.

➢ Another great advantage of Snapchat for business is that the timeline is pretty defined. There is not much clutter that can confuse or distract the audience. Everybody will have their defined space and not have to worry about their snaps getting lost or buried.

Snapchat for Business

It is important to note here that using Snapchat for business will be different from using it as a social media tool to interact with friends and family. You will have to take a different approach to it, as it is important for people to understand that they are interacting with a company and not an individual.

Having said that, it should not be too serious, as it will become a little boring for the audience. It will be important to represent the company in the best possible manner and allow the audience to connect with it.

Here is a step-by-step guide to follow in order to set up the ideal Snapchat profile for your business.

Chapter Six: Snapchat For Business

➢ Step 1: the first step will be to install the app. Follow the same instructions as mentioned in chapter 1.

➢ Step 2: while setting up the account ensure that you make it as professional as possible. Choose your company's name as your Snapchat name so that people know that it is the company's official page. Pick your company's logo to act as your profile picture. For example, Disney uses their logo to go in the center of the ghost. If you don't have a recognizable logo then just add in your company's name to tell people about it.

➢ Step 3: the next step will be to add your friends. This will create an instant audience base for you and ensure that you start on the right foot. They will be able to see what you post and provide you with valuable feedback. Based on it, make the requisite changes to your campaigns and make it interesting for them.

➢ Step 3: Next, find other companies and follow them. This will help you know what they are up to and the type cf strategies that they are using. You will also have to keep track of your advertisers and what they are posting. All of this will go a long way in helping you come up with great promotions for your business.

➢ Step 4: the next step will be to choose and build your audience. This will possibly be the most important step of the process. You will have to accrue as many followers as possible in order to reach out to a large number of people. It is on par with finding as many twitter followers as possible

➢ Step 5: follow some of the most famous stars on Snapchat, as that will help you enhance your audience base. If you know some of them then ask them to add you as well as that will enhance your friend count.

➤ Step 6: next, create snaps and stories that are going to appeal to a large audience. That will help you start right. After a certain point you will have the chance to concentrate on just a small target audience and build strategies to cater to them.

➤ Step 7: make sure you set a fixed time to update your snaps and stories, as people will know when to expect an update. It will be best to

Chapter Seven:

Increasing Snapchat followers

We have by now understood how effective Snapchat can be in terms of enhancing your business. But it will be important for you to build as big a community as possible in order to reach out to as many customers as you can.

Here are some tips and tricks to increase your Snapchat followers.

Post Daily

It is extremely important to post daily and keep your audiences updated. That is the only way to keep them interested and coming back to your page. Think of quirky things that will help you garner their attention and keep them interested in your snaps. Keep track of what some of the other companies are doing and make sure you match up to them. It will be very easy to tap into the market if you pay a little attention to the type of content that sells on Snapchat and use the same to your advantage.

Public Stories

Ensure you make all your stories public. This is important, as people will have to go through what you share. The stories will self-destruct the next day and then you will have to add another one. But if you want to share certain exclusive pictures that only a select few customers can see. This will make them feel special and help you strengthen your bond with them. Some companies tend to make all snaps private, which will work counter productively to the campaign. It will therefore be best to make all of it public.

Other Platforms

A good idea is to link all your social media platforms. This includes linking your Facebook, twitter and Snapchat accounts together and sharing information between them. This will make it more relatable to your audience. Continuing the same campaign on all platforms ensures that there is uniformity and people are able to better connect with it. They will also move from one platform to another thereby making it easy for you to import your contacts. We will look at how to link the different social media platforms with Snapchat in the next chapter.

Expand Contacts

It is understood that Snapchat taps into your contact list and adds friends from it. It will therefore help with the cause to expand your contact list as much as possible in order to reach out to more number of people. Make use of leads and send out messages to friends. They will be able to see your updates and know what is being offered. Don't leave any opportunity to avail someone's number, as you never know who will translate into a customer. Also tap into your friends' and acquaintances friend list in order to expand your following.

Groups

Make sure you join appropriate groups on other forms of social media such as Facebook and twitter. That way, you will remain in contact with all those that can help you expand your business. There will also be forums on the Internet where you can post or update the threads and leave behind your Snapchat name in order to get them to visit your page. Start your own topics there and pick the ones that will sell the most. These groups can also serve as a great platform to get an insight into strategies that some of the others are adopting.

Creativity

It is extremely important to be creative with the content. Redundant pictures and stories will not take you anywhere. They will only make it boring for your audience. It will therefore be important to choose interesting pictures that will be a hit with your audience. You need not always aggressively promote your products. Keep posting pictures that are interesting and appealing. For example if you are a fashion based company then share pictures related to your products but belonging to other sites or blogs. There is no set rule as to what can go up and what cannot. As long as it is connected to your business and capable of garnering attention, it will help you stay in loop.

Variety

Variety is the spice of life. Don't be too predictable with your pictures; pick things that will surprise the audience. Remember to add value to your content. If they get the same thing as what they get elsewhere then it is pretty useless. They have to come to it only because what you are offering is unique. So keep it interesting and unique for the audience, as it will catapult your popularity. Remember that content is king when it comes to social media and extremely important to stay on top with it.

Up to Date

Use up to date content and material for your snaps. They should use the latest lenses and filters available and any other update. Using old and redundant mediums will make it boring for your audience. The numbers will increase if you post viral content that is up to date.

Tie Ups

Consider following some of the popular Snapchatters and get them to follow you. This will increase your followers automatically as theirs will take to you. Look up some of the most popular ones in your area and follow them.

When you email them add your Snapchat code or name at the bottom to prompt them to follow you.

These form the different ways in which one can increase their followers. Each one will help you enhance the count and remain with a large following.

Chapter Eight:

Snapchat and Other Media

S napchat is a great social media tool to keep in touch with friends and followers. But if you already have a lot of them on your other platforms and wish to import them then there are a few things that can be done for it.

Here is looking at what you can do to link your social medias with Snapchat.

Facebook

Facebook is probably where you have a lot of friends and followers on your page. A nice and easy way to get them on board with your Snapchat account is by mentioning your

Snapchat name and code on your Facebook page or account. This will help people find you on Snapchat and add you. This is a convenient way to move people and don't have to put in too much effort towards it.

Twitter

Twitter is another platform where you will have a lot of followers and can easily move them from there to your Snapchat account. Add it to your description so that they can look it up and add you there. You can also mention it in a few of the tweets especially when you are replying to people who have asked you a query about your products or services.

Instagram

Instagram is another place where you will have a lot of followers. Add your Snapchat name to the description that you provide. Many people forget to this assuming others will automatically look them up on Snapchat and follow. But it is extremely important to spoon-feed people information so that they know what to do next.

Google+

It is extremely important for you to not forget about Google+. Many people disregard it assuming it is not as popular as the other platforms but should not be discounted. Mention your Snapchat name in your Google+ description. You also have the option of mentioning it at the end of an email to notify the receiver about the same.

LinkedIn

LinkedIn is another place to avail potential followers. If you have many connections then mention your Snapchat name in your description so that they can look you up and follow. LinkedIn helps connect you to many potential business partners and that will allow you to expand your network.

Blogs/websites

It will also be best to include your Snapchat name or Snapcode in your blogs and websites. Add it at the bottom of every post so that people notice it and follow you. If you make use of visiting cards then have your Snapcode or Snapchat name added to it in order to tell people about the same. Remember, you will have to indulge in self-promotion in order to get noticed.

Hire team

If you have a big following then it will pay to employ a team to take care of your Snapchat account. The team can update the account on a regular basis in order to make it interesting for your audiences. Look for people that have relevant experience in the field and be in a position to update with eye catching and interesting content. You must also check their previous work to see if they make for the right candidates to join your team.

These are the simple ways in which you can transfer people. It is important to do so as it will pay to have a sizeable list of followers on your Snapchat account. There are also many other benefits that will come your way when you import your contacts over.

Chapter Nine:
Snapchat Marketing
Strategies

S napchat is a great platform for you to market your products and services. Here is looking at some Snapchat strategies to try in order to enhance your business.

Contests

Organizing exclusive contests on your Snapchat is a great idea. People will be able to partake in them and relate better. The contests can be anything like choosing a caption for your pictures or putting up pictures with the product. All of these are great ways to promote your Snapchat account and market products. The giveaway after the contest ends should be unique or worthy so that people put in their best efforts. Announce about the contest on all your different social media platforms in advance so that people know when to take part in it.

Events

Announce events for your customers through Snapchat. The platform provides a great opportunity to bring your customers together. Post invites for them and ask them to screenshot it. Whoever has it can appear at the event. This makes for a great way to engage the audience and get them to RSVP to the event. Again, announce about it on all your social media platforms so that people known about it in advance. Ask them at the event whether they liked the concept and would like to have more of it. Plan your future campaigns based on their response.

Tie Ups

It is a good idea to tie up with other companies on Snapchat. Doing so will help you exchange followers. For example, post a picture and ask your followers to screenshot it. The same can work as a coupon to avail discount for your partner's products and vice versa. But remember to tie up with companies that have equal or more number of followers as you as that will be fair game. Once you have a successful run you will be able to tie up with others with much ease. You need not limit it to just one partner and tie up with as many as you like.

Offers

Provide exclusive discounts and other offers on your Snapchat only. This can be something like coupon codes to avail discount, buy one get one free etc. These offers should be exclusively available on your Snapchat account alone and not anywhere else. But you can advertise about it on your other platforms in order to tell your customers about the same. Try to vary the offers every now and then in order to keep the audience engaged. Look at what some of the offers by rival companies and match up to it. Again, come up with innovative ways to announce the offers on your Snapchat account.

Previews

Snapchat is a great place for you to offer a sneak peak into your upcoming products and services. Add a picture or video of what is to come and your audience will be at the edge of their seat. Incorporate a game here also and make it interesting. Ask them to take a screenshot of a particular product from the newest collection that they can win. Similarly, think up other ways in which to market your products using Snapchat to reach out to a bigger audience.

Media Exclusives

A nice trick to increase followers is to offer exclusive products through Snapchat alone. For example, only your followers on Snapchat will have access to a particular collection. These can be different in terms of color, design or pattern. You will have to tell them clearly that they will be exclusively available through Snapchat alone and not anywhere else. Consider introducing a whole different line of products that are only available through your Snapchat account.

Merchandize

Offer customers exclusive merchandize. These will carry your company's name and logo. You also have the choice to add their name or any other information that they would like to have on the merchandize. Customizing products for customers help them keep coming for more and Snapchat can play a part in it.

Celebrities

Celebrities work like magic in terms of garnering attention. Start following celebrities and get them to follow you. This will create a buzz about your company. Keep your best friend list open for people see, as they will know who is on your list. The same extends to having popular Snapchatters on your list. Others will be able to see who you have and enhance your account's appeal. There are many fashion models to follow. It will be great if you get one of them to wear or use your products and use the same in your account.

Rewards

Offer your customers rewards such as incentives for following your Snapchat account. That will ensure you increase the number of followers. The rewards can be discount coupons or store credit that the followers can use to avail discounts and other offers. Announce the same in advance and on other platforms as well.

Referrals

Offer rewards for referrals as well. This is a trick that many businesses now use to attract followers. Announce a reward for those that bring in other followers. The reward should be lucrative enough to attract people and keep them interested.

These form the different ways in which you can tap into Snapchat's marketing potential. All of these are great but can pick the ones that work best for your company.

Chapter Ten:

Snapchat Lenses, Filters and Settings

S napchat is an app meant to help people have fun with their pictures and videos. One of the prominent features of Snapchat is the lens that can be used to enhance a picture's quality.

Here is looking at the feature in detail.

Snapchat lenses are quite easy to add to pictures, all you need to do is press and hold the picture and the app will automatically determine where to place the filter. This makes your job easier as you do not have to place the filters manually. Remember that these filters can be placed on both snaps and videos.

Chapter Ten: Snapchat Lenses, Filters and Settings

Here are some of the common lenses used

- ➤ A flower crown is placed on top of the head to look like a wreath.

- ➤ A butterfly crown is placed on the head.

- ➤ A face swap allows you to swap faces with a contact on your list or a friend.

- ➤ The dog filter places dog ears and nose on your face.

- ➤ The rainbow vomit filter places a rainbow over your mouth.

These lenses make it extremely interesting and fun for your audiences. Although Snapchat automatically places the lenses on top of your pictures it will be easier if you make the same face as is on the lens. For example, opening your mouth wide will help the app place the rainbow lens correctly.

Filters

Filters help you write on top of a picture or video. It also provides a place to add a caption or tagline. This is useful, as it will tell the other person what you are trying to do in the picture.

Just like with a lens you can swipe right or left to find the filter of choice and place it on top of the picture or video. Once there, fill in whatever you want to add as the caption.

Check filters

It can sometimes get confusing when you have to pick between two great filters. For this, test both and settle for the one you think suits the picture best. For example press the screen and use to place two filters before choosing the one that stays. This is great for all those that cannot choose between two or more filters. You can also place stickers on your pictures. Just click on the emoji option next to the T and add it to the picture on top.

Chapter Ten: Snapchat Lenses, Filters and Settings

Emojis

The emojis on Snapchat are extremely versatile and there are many to choose from. Apart from adding them to your pictures and videos they can also be added to objects in your pictures. This means that you need not pin the emojis to people alone and can also go on objects that are there in it. This makes the photos and videos a little more personal and interesting for the viewers. They can be pinned wherever you would like them to be on the picture or video.

Colors

Many people wonder as to why there is no black and white in the color palette whereas all other pictures are available. But don't worry as a simple trick can help you remain with both of these colors. Use your finger to drag it to the left top corner to remain with white color. Use it to draw or write over the picture or video. Drag it to the bottom left of the page to remain with black and use it to write on the picture or video using black color.

Songs

Songs and music are a big part of Snapchat videos. They enhance the quality and feel of the videos. Although Snapchat does not have a add audio feature, it is pretty simple to incorporate music into your videos. All you have to do is go to any of the music playing apps and play the song you wish to incorporate. Record the video with the music playing in the background and Snapchat will record and add it to the background.

Music

It is also possible for you to turn off the music. Not everybody likes to have music and songs play in their snaps and videos. In order to switch it off, record the video with the sound, as that will be an option. Now you will find the volume option at the bottom shaped like a loudspeaker.

Chapter Ten: Snapchat Lenses, Filters and Settings

Press once to switch it off and an X will appear in front of it to signify that the volume has been turned off. Thee video will now not play the sound when it is viewed.

Chapter Eleven:

Snapchat Tips and Tricks

Here is looking at some Snapchat tips and tricks to follow.

Snapchat Discover

Snapchat discover is a unique feature on Snapchat designed to help you keep tab of magazines, websites and other such channels that you wish to follow. Snapchat helps in providing all the different channels and apps in one place so that you don't have to download the individual apps. Right from cosmopolitan to Buzzfeed to MTV, there is a lot to choose from and clicking on them will give you all the latest news and gossip. You will also be able to access live stories and other such fun content without having to leave the app. You don't have to always click on the individual apps and can press it down to subscribe to the individual channels. The latest news from the site will automatically update without you having to manually look for it. This feature makes it extremely convenient for people to keep track of all the latest events and happenings around them. All the features are professionally curated to make it look great. You will have the chance to use it as inspiration and come up with great content yourself to share with friends and followers.

Updating

You have the choice to manually update Snapchat if you like. Although it generally updates automatically, you can manually look for any updates on the play store. Click the update button to do the needful and your Snapchat will be updated. If you are unable to do so then move to your settings and check if you have chosen to receive automatic updates. If not, then enable the option to automatically update your Snapchat.

Secret Screenshot

Secretly screenshot another person's pictures without them knowing about it. Here are the steps to follow for the same.

- ➢ Start by loading the snap but don't open it. If it has automatically loaded then do not open it.

- ➢ Once you load the image, go to notifications and switch on the airplane mode.

- ➢ Once airplane mode is on tap the Snapchat button and open it. Screenshot using the same method as usual.

- ➢ Now exit the app and ensure it is not running in the background. iOS users can double click on the home button and swipe the app to close it. Android users can do this in the multitasking window and close it.

> Now deactivate airplane mode and close Snapchat. You can now open Snapchat and carry on as usual.

Assign Numbers

It is obvious that we will have a few best friends in our lists. This refers to those that we regularly message. You have the option of changing their numbers in order to message them easily. Snapchat automatically assigns numbers to the ones that you message regularly. It generally assigns the number 3 but this can be changed to a 5 or 7 depending on what you would like to assign to it. This will make it easier for you to message these people without looking for them in your friend list.

Deleting Account

If for some reason you do not wish to maintain your account owing to security reasons then you have the choice to delete it. Login to your account and choose the delete option. This will delete your account for good. You will again be able to create another account using a different username. But remember, once you delete your account, it cannot be undone and you cannot revive the same. You will have to create a new one that will be different from your old account and carry a different username.

Travel Mode

You have the option of picking travel mode on your Snapchat account in order to prevent automatic download of pictures and videos. This is great for all those whose phone batteries tend to drain away fast. Performing this simple trick can help you save on battery life and not have to worry about unwanted pictures downloading on your phone. Choose the ones you wish to download and get stored on your phone. To enable the travel mode go to settings and then to "manage". There you will find the option of "additional services" where you will find travel mode. Click on it to enable it.

Deleting Snaps

It is possible for you to delete a single snap from a story. This is useful for all those that tend to add in several pictures and then trim it down to size. For this, choose the picture you would like to delete and swipe it upwards. The delete button will appear on top and pressing it will remove that particular picture from the story. A pop up will ask if you surely want to delete the picture and choosing delete again will make the snap disappear.

Content from outside Snapchat

Now you may wonder if you are only allowed to upload those snaps and videos on Snapchat that were created using Snapchat tools. The answer is *no*, you don't have to rely on Snapchat alone to create your snaps and videos. It is also possible for you to upload content that was created using external apps. There are many third party apps available that will help you create snaps and videos using your camera and then save it to your camera roll. The same can be uploaded to your Snapchat account. One such popular external app is snap upload. However, it is important to remember that this is not how Snapchat is supposed to be used. It is a place to upload raw pictures that are not touched up or photo shopped. It will be best to keep it that way as real pictures are more appreciated than altered ones.

Reusing Snaps

It is possible for you to make use of old snaps and videos and repost them with new content such as lenses and filters. This will be helpful for those that want to keep it interesting and unique but don't have the time to take new pictures. All you have to do is tap on the download arrow once the snap has been taken. This will save the picture for you. If you wish to download an entire story then head over to the dots on the right of the story screen and choose the download button to download the story. Once done, add any filters and lens you like or modify it in any other way you like before uploading it.

Tips for Great Snaps

Here are some general tips on how you can make your snaps look clear and nice.

Camera

First and foremost get yourself a quality smartphone with a good quality camera. It is important to have a front facing camera, as you will be able to see the snap being taken. Although a good back camera with flash will also work, you will have to take multiple snaps to pick the best one. If you will be using Snapchat to promote your products and services then it will be best to do some research on the best phone or tablet to pick. You also have the option of using a good quality external camera to take the pictures and then upload to your Snapchat account.

Lighting

The next aspect to bear in mind is the lighting. The lighting can play a big part in making or breaking the perfect picture. You have to take the picture in a bright spot. But make sure it is not too bright, as it will create a bright light on your face. Trial and error is a must in order to find the right angle and lighting for your face. Nothing beats sunlight or natural light as it provides just the right amount of brightness. If you are trying to photograph an object then place it in an appropriate place before taking the picture.

Expressions

It is important to pay attention to your expressions. Some people put on a face for the camera and fail to provide a genuine expression. It will be important to provide a genuine expression to the camera as Snapchat is meant to capture the moment. There is no rule in maintaining a certain kind of smile. Smile however you like as long as it is genuine. Apart from smiling, experiment with your expressions and try to capture the moment as best as possible. Work with the angles of your face and pick the one that is best.

Editors

Make use of editors to enhance picture quality. There are many external apps available that can be used to edit a picture. These editors are mostly used to fix the brightness, color and texture of a picture. Sharpness and blurriness can also be fixed using the same. You do not have to make too many changes and make it look completely different. Just touching the pictures up will help you upload nice pictures.

Filters and lens

The last step is to make use of filters and lenses. These will help a picture look unique and fun. We already looked at what they can add to a picture and that there are many options to pick from. Choose whatever you think will look best.

These form the different criteria to bear in mind while taking the perfect snap.

These are especially important for those that wish to monetize their account. For that, you have to upload good quality pictures able to captivate the imagination of people and potential advertisers.

Here is how you can do to monetize your Snapchat account.

1. Step 1: The first step is to create content that will grab eyeballs. This can range from trying on makeup products to sporting clothes and accessories to reviewing products.

2. Step 2: the next step is to get noticed by companies that will sponsor your pictures and videos.

3. Step 3: once they approach you, look at the terms and conditions they have and go through all of it in detail. Once you are

satisfied with it, you can sign up with them.

4. Step 4: they will provide the basis for videos and snaps they expect from you. You will have to adhere to their requirements and upload the same.

5. Step 5: you will be paid for your work based on the agreement you have with them.

6. This is a great way to monetize if you have a large number of followers following your Snapchat account.

Chapter Twelve:

How Snapchat Can Improve

Although Snapchat is a great platform to promote business activities, it has a few shortcomings. Here is looking at some areas where Snapchat can improve to provide a better experience.

Exclusive

Although Snapchat is not designed to serve as a platform for businesses to promote their products and services, it will be great to have a business exclusive Snapchat. The app can have a separate interface for businesses so that it is easier for them to use. The option to move people from other media platforms will also be extremely convenient, as they will have to put in lesser effort to generate a following. The platform can also help find advertisers and other potential business entities that can help to promote business. The app will be easier to maintain and keep up with, as there will be only businesses on it.

Engagement

Since the current version is not designed for business houses, the engagement level for audiences is quite low. People do not make the effort to go through what a business house is posting and treat it as a mere update. This will be different for an exclusive Snapchat for business app. Audience engagement will enhance and make it fun for people to go through the snaps and stories. Managing content will become much easier as people will not have to worry about creating content for a specific audience and make big scale advertising projects.

Time Frame

The 24-hour limit can be a hindrance for some companies, as they would have worked hard on a campaign. Once it disappears, they will have to upload the same again. This can get monotonous and tiring. The business exclusive app can be modified to help pictures stay for longer. It need not be too long, as people get bored easily. A one-week window with an extension of two or three days seems ideal, as a majority of the audience would have seen the campaign by then. People will also know when to expect the next update and wait on it. This enhances business potential and makes it predictable for a business to plan the campaigns well.

Policies

Certain policies can be introduced that will invite more and more companies to partake in the advertising aspect of Snapchat. Trust will come in, which will make it easier for businesses to use it to advertise their products and services without worrying about trivial details. An agreement policy at the beginning will work, as it will enhance user experience. Providing them with some form of guarantee towards helping them increase their reach and sales will prove to be a big hit.

Safety

Safety is another concern that worries many who sign up with Snapchat. This can be a problem for a business, as getting hacked can serve as a hindrance. There is also the issue with copyrights. All of these need to be taken care of in order to make it ideal for businesses. Providing additional security features will prove to be a big attraction for companies. It will especially attract bigger companies for whom secrecy and security can be a big deal.

Content

There has been worry over content that is not verified or not suitable for a certain audience.

This can prove to be a hindrance for advertising campaigns as people will disregard it or treat it as spam. There needs to be a little more control and filter to separate the spam. Small companies will benefit from this feature, as their content will be more visible. It will also prevent aggressive advertising, which is no longer encouraged or loved by the audiences.

Interface

The interface of the app can be further enhanced by providing more features and organizing them in a better manner. A professional will require professional tools to work with in order to come up with the best advertising campaigns. Although the current features are good they are mostly for teens and young adults. They do not provide a good opportunity for businesses to advertise effectively. Incorporating some of the features from other advertising apps and software will help enhance Snapchat's value for businesses.

Community

Snapchat business can establish a feeling of community. A business can keep track of another and follow in its footsteps. It can also have first hand knowledge of what they are up to. This will promote healthy competition and ensure everybody finds his or her space. This is especially important for small businesses, as there is the danger of their content getting lost. If there is community support, then campaigns will find it easier to survive and be seen by more number of people. Companies can also form specific groups and further boost viewership.

Communication

The current version of the app does not allow people to reach out to companies or businesses. It is also difficult to get across a call to action message making it tough for people to respond to an ad campaign. People need to be told what to do in order to get them to buy products and services. This option is available on most other social media platforms where people have the chance to click on a link and get redirected to the company website. The same needs to be incorporated on Snapchat, as companies will be able to market themselves better.

These form the different ways in which Snapchat can improve. It is certain that they will introduce some of these changes in the upcoming updates to help incorporate more business houses.

Summary

napchat is the perfect app to use to keep in touch with friends and family members. It is designed to help you share all your latest photos and videos and keep them updated about your life. Snapchat is a social media app but with a small difference. It is exclusively meant to share pictures and videos that last a short period of time. Once shared, they will remain only for 1 to 10 seconds and then get destroyed. You have the choice to pick the time period for which the snaps will be available to the receiver. This makes it extremely safe and secure.

It was launched in 2011 with the intention of helping people capture the moment they are in and share it with others. This forms the very basis of the app, as it is meant to capture a raw

Summary

emotion in real time. Snapchat taps into your phone contacts and allows you add whomever you want to your friend list. Once done, they will be able to see your snaps and videos and you will be able to see theirs. Apart from the people in your friend list, you can also have followers. These are people who have added you to their list. It is extremely easy to get started with Snapchat. It can be downloaded from the app store and installed on your phone. Once done, you will have to fill in some details before using the app.

There are many options present on the screen such as taking a snap, uploading a snap, taking a video, uploading a video, making a video call, texting etc. All of these are great quality features. There are a few terms that you have to know in order to use Snapchat. These include the likes of Snapchatters, snaps, snapbacks, friends, followers etc. Knowing these terms can help you Snapchat in a better way. The latest version of Snapchat provides you with some amazing features. They are designed to please even a wide range of people including college goers and working professionals. These new features are explained in detail in this book and you can go through them once again to know what is in store for you.

There are a few tips and tricks to follow in order to come up with the perfect snaps and videos to upload to your account. Some of them include picking the right camera, focusing on the lighting, editing the pictures, making use of lenses and filters etc. it will be important to upload the perfect snaps in order to enhance followers. There are many other ways in which to increase followers. You will have to put in the requisite effort to increase your followers. The more you have the easier it will be to monetize.

Although Snapchat is extremely popular among teens and young adults, it is also a good platform for companies to promote their business. There are many ways in which a company can use Snapchat to promote its products and services.

Summary

One of the best ways is to post pictures of products that people can expect at the store. This creates a buzz and can help enhance sales.

It is also a great tool for advertising. There are many different ways in which Snapchat can be used to advertise products and services. Some of them include hosting competitions, organizing events etc.

Although Snapchat is a great platform to share snaps and videos, there are a few places where it can improve. Having a Snapchat exclusively for business purposes will make for a great option.

Conclusion

I thank you once again for choosing this book and hope you had fun reading it.

The main aim of this book was to educate you on the basics of Snapchat and teach you how it can be used to your advantage. You must have learnt a lot of new things through this book and are raring to put it to practice. It is ideal for businesses to increase their customer base and enhance sales. In fact, Snapchat can work like a charm in helping you improve your business on many levels.

I hope you fulfill all your wishes by making use of this app.

Good luck!